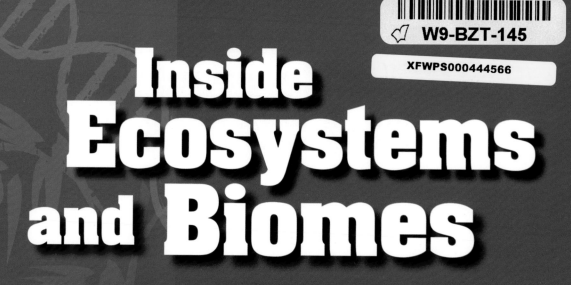

Inside
Ecosystems
and Biomes

Debra J. Housel, M.S.Ed.

Life Science Readers:
Inside Ecosystems and Biomes

Publishing Credits

Editorial Director
Dona Herweck Rice

Associate Editor
Joshua BishopRoby

Editor-in-Chief
Sharon Coan, M.S.Ed.

Creative Director
Lee Aucoin

Illustration Manager
Timothy J. Bradley

Publisher
Rachelle Cracchiolo, M.S.Ed.

Science Contributor
Sally Ride Science™

Science Consultants
Thomas R. Ciccone, B.S., M.A. Ed.
Chino Hills High School
Dr. Ronald Edwards,
DePaul University

Teacher Created Materials
5301 Oceanus Drive
Huntington Beach, CA 92649-1030
http://www.tcmpub.com
ISBN 978-0-7439-0591-6

Table of Contents

What Is an Ecosystem? 4

Earth's Land Biomes.. 10

Earth's Water Biomes... 22

You and Your Ecosystem 26

Appendices 28

    Lab: Creating an Algae Bloom 28

    Glossary 30

    Index 31

    Sally Ride Science... 32

    Image Credits 32

What Is an Ecosystem?

Jackrabbits live in the Mojave Desert. You might think that there isn't much life in the middle of the desert. The jackrabbit knows better. Every day, the jackrabbit finds plants to eat. It eats sagebrush, mesquite, and even cactus! It also has to watch out for **predators**. Coyotes and eagles eat jackrabbits.

There is a lot of life in the jackrabbit's world. All the living things in the Mojave Desert depend on one another to survive. The jackrabbit needs the plants. The coyotes need jackrabbits to eat. And even the plants need the animals. Together, the plants and animals form an **ecosystem**. An ecosystem includes all the plants and animals that need one another.

The number of plants and animals must stay balanced. Too many jackrabbits will eat the plants faster than they can grow back. Too many coyotes will run out of food as well.

jackrabbit

Scientists observed what happened when a pair of moose swam out to an island called Isle Royale. Within 10 years, there were 3,000 moose! But there weren't enough plants to eat, so they started to die. Then a pair of wolves arrived. Eating the moose made their numbers grow. But soon there were too many wolves, and they starved. At last, 600 moose and 20 wolves lived on the island. This was just enough to keep them both from starving.

Isle Royale

moose

wolves

increased
size

decreased
energy

increased
size

decreased
energy

All ecosystems have energy pyramids within them. One energy pyramid is illustrated above. It shows the exchange of energy from one food source to another.

Plants are at the bottom of most energy pyramids. In fact, without plants, there would be no life on Earth as we know it. Plants use light from the sun for **photosynthesis**. This lets them make and store energy. They also use nutrients from the soil.

Animals are **consumers**. A gazelle and a zebra eat some grass. They take the energy and nutrients from the grass and use it to run, eat, and mate. Later, a lion eats the gazelle and zebra. It will use the energy and nutrients in them. The gazelle and zebra had already used some of the energy, and the lion takes the rest. As you can see, the overall energy drops as the size of the consumer increases.

Eventually, the lion dies. **Decomposers** break down the lion's remains. These worms, bacteria, and fungi use the energy and return the nutrients to the soil. When plants use these nutrients, a new energy pyramid begins.

Most of the energy is lost at each step in the pyramid. Just a fraction of the sunlight that reaches plants is turned into energy. Animal consumers use only 10 to 20 percent of the energy in their food.

Omnivores Are Common

Not long ago, scientists learned a new fact: many animals are omnivores. Most animals were once called herbivores or carnivores. Herbivores eat plants. Carnivores eat meat. Omnivores eat both. In fact, it's hard to think of an animal that only eats plants. Mice, ostriches, grasshoppers, and even deer sometimes eat meat!

This also shows that ecosystems are more complex than scientists had thought. An animal that you might think of as a herbivore may also sometimes eat meat. We once thought of ecosystems having food chains, but that is usually too simple. Most ecosystems have food webs, with most organisms eating many different things.

Earth has different areas called **biomes**. Each biome has its own **climate**. For example, a desert has dry weather and sand or rocks instead of soil. This affects the kinds of plants and animals that can live there.

Altitude and **latitude** determine biome boundaries. Altitude measures how high a place is. Latitude helps determine how hot a place is.

Altitude measures the height above sea level. It affects what can grow. For example, trees will only grow up to the tree line on a mountain. Above that, it is too windy and cold. Most of the soil has blown away, leaving only rocks. Only short plants can grow in this alpine biome. Sheep, elk, chinchillas, and birds live here and eat these plants.

Latitude measures the distance from the **equator**. The equator is an invisible line around the middle of Earth. The closer a place is to the equator, the hotter the weather. The farther away from the equator, the cooler the weather gets.

The plant life and climate of an area can tell you something about its altitude and latitude.

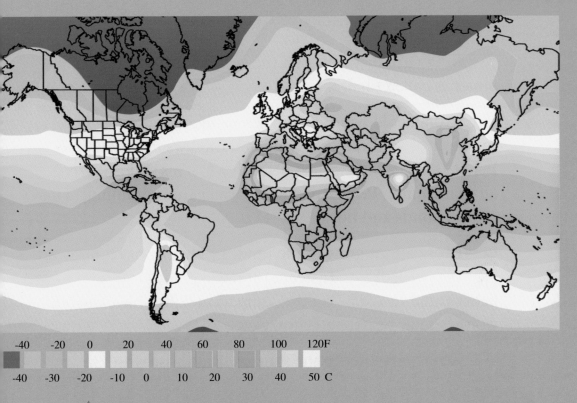

-40	-20	0	20	40	60	80	100	120F
-40	-30	-20	-10	0	10	20	30	40	50 C

You can see how the different biomes look like they are stacked on top of each other, shown as stripes around the planet. The closer to the equator, the warmer it gets. Warm biomes are close to the equator. Colder biomes are near the poles.

In the far north, summers are too short and cool for trees. Only short grass, lichens, and mosses grow in the tundra biome. These plants can do photosynthesis at low temperatures with long spells of daylight. Caribou eat the grasses and polar bears may eat the caribou.

polar bears

Tundra

At the top of the world, the weather is very cold. This biome is called **tundra**.

Strong, cold winds sweep across the flat tundra. The top layer of soil freezes in winter and thaws in the summer. Below that is a layer called **permafrost**. This soil is frozen all year round. Permafrost keeps water from draining. This creates ponds and bogs.

Trees cannot grow in the tundra. Their roots cannot get past the permafrost. Instead, tundra regions grow grasses, lichens, and mosses. Tundra animals include voles, caribou, wolves, polar bears, and snowy owls.

Few people live on the tundra. But those who do, need heat. When heat escapes from buildings, roads, and pipelines, it can thaw the permafrost. **Global warming** also melts permafrost, creating more bogs than there should be. During the past 100 years, the permafrost has retreated about 50 miles north.

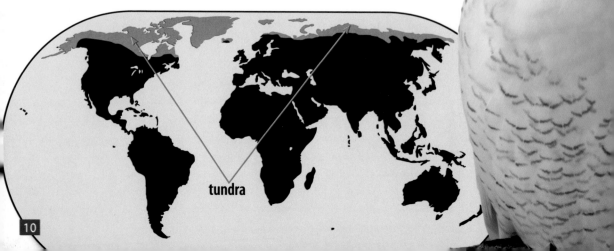

tundra

Caribou!

You probably think of these animals as reindeer. When they run wild, they are known as caribou. Caribou travel in herds across the tundra. They eat lichen and grasses. Sometimes they eat birds and voles, so they are omnivores. They travel in herds for protection from wolves and polar bears. To stay warm, caribou have two layers of fur.

A Tiny Tundra Dweller

The arctic ground squirrel spends most of its life asleep in a burrow just above the permafrost. While it sleeps, it lives off its layer of fat. When the squirrel wakes up, it has 90 days to mate, raise its young, and eat enough food to build a fat layer. To do this, it must work at least 17 hours a day! Then it curls up for another nine-month nap.

← snowy owl

Taiga

Just south of the tundra is the largest land biome. It is called **taiga**. Winters are long and cold. Summers are short and cool.

Evergreen trees can grow in the taiga. They do not lose their leaves in the winter. Animals that need trees can live in taiga, too. Birds nest in the trees. Deer hide in the shade.

The taiga covers much of Canada, Russia, and China. Grizzly bears, eagles, deer, and bats make their homes in these pine forests. This environment also has lakes, bogs, and rivers.

taiga

black bear ➡

Protecting the Original Taiga

Most of the Russian Federation is covered by taiga. In fact, the word *taiga* comes from Russia. It means cold forest. Russia's taiga is home to arctic foxes, brown bears, musk deer, and snow leopards. Unfortunately, this unique region faces serious threats. Poachers hunt the animals illegally. Loggers also break the law to cut down trees. The climate is changing because of nearby cities. The Russians don't want to lose their taiga. They have turned almost four million hectares of taiga into protected land.

Black Bear

Some black bears live in the taiga. They eat salmon, fawns, and rodents. They also eat berries, leaves, and even ants! Because it's so cold in the taiga, bears have to eat anything they can to keep warm. Food adds layers of fat that help them to keep warm. Black bears are also big and strong. They are so big that no other animal hunts adult bears. This makes them **apex predators**. Such a predator would appear at the top of an energy pyramid.

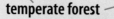

temperate forest

Peregrine Falcon

The peregrine falcon is the fastest animal on the planet. It soars high into the air and then dives toward the ground. This is called a stoop. It can go as fast as 300km/h (185 mph)! The falcon uses the stoop to hunt. It mostly hunts other birds. It snatches them right out of the air. Peregrine falcons hunt doves and ducks in the wilderness. Some falcons have moved into big cities. They live on top of skyscrapers and hunt pigeons!

young peregrine falcon

Temperate Forest

A little farther south, the weather warms up. There are four seasons instead of just two. This is the **temperate forest**.

Some trees and shrubs in the temperate forest have learned a neat trick. They lose their leaves each fall. The leaves are used to gather lots of sunlight during the spring and summer. The plant stores the energy and uses it through the winter. It gets rid of the leaves when it doesn't need them. Plants that shed their leaves are called **deciduous**. Maple, beech, and oak trees are common examples.

Deer, raccoons, foxes, rabbits, and squirrels make their homes in these forests. Many people do, too. In fact, people have cut down most of these forests for homes, farms, and orchards. Now people all over the world are replanting trees to replace the forests.

Working Together to Save the Pandas

The giant panda, found only in China, needs a special kind of forest to live. It is a bamboo forest. Much of the pandas' forests have been cut down. At first, China made it illegal to cut down the forest or hunt the animals in the ecosystem. The local people needed food to eat and wood to burn for heat. They broke into the reserves even though it was illegal.

Now China is working to find ways for the locals to be part of the ecosystem, too. Locals are allowed to have farms that don't hurt the ecosystem. They use stoves that burn *biogas* (gas made from the decay of living matter) instead of wood. Now the pandas and their forests should be safe.

tropical rainforest

Tropical Rainforest

Near the equator, the average temperature is near 77°F year-round. It rains all the time. This is where you will find **tropical rainforests**. The Amazon Rainforest in South America is the world's largest. Others can be found in Central America, Asia, Africa, and Australia.

Tropical rainforests have *millions* of different plants and animals. They cover less than 7 percent of the land on the planet. Yet they support more than half the Earth's plant and animal species! The plants and trees there soak up carbon dioxide. Since this is one of the gases that cause global warming, these forests help to reduce the problem.

Good Luck Gekko

Most reptiles are quiet. Not the tokay gekko. It chirps its own name: "Tokay! Gek gek!" Gekkos come from the rainforest. They climb up trees using their sticky feet. They use their long tongues to snatch insects out of the air. In Southeast Asia, many people let gekkos live in their houses! The gekkos climb up the walls and eat bugs. Some people say they bring good luck.

At the top of a rainforest is a **canopy** of tree branches that overlap each other. Little sunlight gets through. Plants on the forest floor have adapted. Many have leaves with deep red coloring to use whatever light reaches them. Other plants trap and eat bugs!

People have destroyed a lot of the rainforests. They have cut down trees for logging, mining, and furniture making. They have built roads, houses, farms, and oil wells. In just the past 30 years, about 20 percent of all the rainforests have been cleared. Scientists think that *dozens* of rainforest species become **extinct** daily.

The Comeback of the Hyacinth Macaw

This beautiful blue bird almost became extinct. It was so pretty that it became a very popular pet. Thousands of hyacinth macaws were captured in Brazil. They were sold illegally.

At the same time, Brazilian farmers were cutting down trees to plant fields. The macaws needed the trees for nests. There were only 2,000 birds left. Then, some Brazilians decided to save the hyacinth macaw. They nailed boxes to the tops of telephone poles. The birds were fooled. They thought the poles were trees and made their nests inside the boxes. People also convinced farmers to keep some trees for the birds. Now farmers are proud to have hyacinth macaws on their farms.

grassland

Grassland

The **grassland** is a biome found in areas with hot, dry summers and mild, wet winters. This environment can be found in parts of the United States, Mexico, and Chile, and in much of Australia and South Africa. Grasslands cover one-fourth of Earth's land. Every continent has them, except for Antarctica.

In Africa, zebras and giraffes graze on the grasslands. Buffalo once lived on the North American plains, or grasslands. Now sheep and cattle have replaced them. All over the world, people have turned grasslands into farms to grow grain.

Grasslands have evergreen bushes that never grow over 10 feet tall. In some places, these shrubs grow so close together that it's hard to pass through the area.

Keep Your Eyes Peeled

The Meadow Argus butterfly lives in the outback of Australia. Like other butterflies, it eats nectar from flowers. It needs to keep an eye out for birds and other predators. Luckily, the Meadow Argus has a couple extra—eyes, that is. The black spots on its wings fool predators. They think the spots are eyes. This makes the butterfly look much larger and more dangerous. If it works, the predator will look for food that looks less dangerous.

It does not rain often in grasslands. Lightning strikes can start wild fires that rage across the land. Fires happen often. In fact, the plants depend on them. Fires clear the area and release minerals back into the soil. After a fire, seeds quickly sprout. Grass can sprout from its root system, so it starts to grow again soon after the fire.

Elephants vs. Chili Powder

In Nambia, Africa, farmers had a problem with elephants. Hungry elephants would crash through any fence to get at the crops in their fields. The farmers tried everything. They built stronger fences. They rang bells to scare the elephants. They used barbed wire. Nothing could stop the elephants. The farmers had to think of a better way.

Then, someone put up a fence made of ropes tied to poles. The farmers laughed. That wouldn't stop an elephant! But the elephants stayed away. They didn't crash through the ropes. The farmers wanted to know why. The ropes had been dipped in hot chilis. The elephants didn't like the smell. Now all the farmers grow a little patch of chilis to scent their own fences and keep the elephants away.

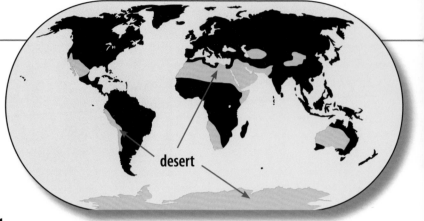

desert

Desert

Some places on Earth hardly ever get rain. Mountains block the winds that bring rain clouds, and the land is dry. This biome is called **desert**.

Most deserts are hot. During the day, the sun scorches the land. It may reach 121°F (50°C) in the shade! Then at night, the temperature drops close to freezing. Desert plants have adapted to these harsh conditions. Some have long water-seeking roots. Others, such as cacti, store water in their stems and roots. Their sharp needles keep animals from getting too much of this water.

To avoid the heat, most desert animals sleep during the day. At night, they come out and look for food. Some desert animals such as camels can store water in their bodies. Others, like burrowing owls, get liquid from the animals they eat. The Thorny Devil in Australia sits outside and lets dew collect on its body. Its skin sucks the moisture to its mouth!

The World's Deserts

Continent	Deserts
Africa	Sahara (largest on Earth) and Kalahari Deserts
Asia	Gobi Desert in China; Arabian and Iranian Deserts in the Middle East
Australia	Great Victoria and Great Sandy Deserts
North America	Mojave, Painted and Baja Deserts in U.S. and Mexico
South America	Patagonia Desert in Argentina
Antarctica	Entire continent (it never rains or snows!)

Meerkats

Meerkats are small rodents that live in Africa's Kalahari Desert. They have to eat every day. They dig up insects, steal eggs, and eat scorpions—stingers and all. They may be small, but meerkats work together. A group of meerkats is called a mob. When the mob goes to get food, one meerkat watches for hawks. He barks when he sees one. Everyone hides until he stops barking. One or two meerkats also stay behind to babysit the mob's young. The rest of the time, meerkats play with one another. They wrestle and race one another around their burrow.

Earth's Water Biomes

Riparian Biomes

People can drink freshwater but not saltwater. All land animals need freshwater, too. Although Earth is covered by mostly water, only 3 percent of it is fresh. And most of that is trapped in polar ice! Therefore, **riparian** biomes are precious. They have running freshwater. Rivers, lakes, and estuaries are all riparian biomes. They support fish, ducks, frogs, and turtles as well as cattails and water plants.

Wetlands are also riparian biomes. They include bogs with soggy soil and marshes that have standing water for part of the year. Swamps always have very slow-moving water. Wetlands are important because they store water and stop floods. Some plants and animals only live in wetlands, like salamanders and

↑ raccoons

lligators. Yet people have drained or filled n thousands of acres of wetlands in order o build homes, farms, and businesses.

Algae blooms occur when **fertilizer** runs off from lawns and farms and collects n lakes or ponds. The blooms reduce he depth to which light can reach. Even worse, the algae lowers the oxygen levels in he water. Without oxygen, fish cannot live.

Mosquito Menace

Mosquitoes breed out of control when wetlands are drained. Why? Mosquitoes will keep breeding in rain puddles and leftover ponds. Without wetlands, there are no homes for predators that eat mosquitoes! When a 1,500-acre (607 hectares) wetland is restored, the number of mosquitoes falls 90 percent!

New York Cleans Up Its Act

New York City is built on the banks of the Hudson River. The river was the reason people built the city there in the first place. Over time, though, people made some poor decisions and polluted the river. Factories dumped bleach and other chemicals into the water. People said it might as well be an open sewer. So they decided to clean it up. They stopped factories from being built on the river. They found ways to take the chemicals back out of the water. Now there are more plants and animals living in the river. The Hudson has gone from a sewer to a beautiful river again.

great white herons

Pelagic Biomes

Salt water covers almost 75 percent of Earth. Oceans, seas, and coral reefs are all **pelagic** biomes. These biomes support life of all shapes and sizes, from microscopic plants and animals to the blue whale, which is the largest animal on Earth. Marine algae supply much of the world's oxygen and absorb huge amounts of carbon dioxide.

Coral reefs are colorful biomes found in warm, shallow parts of the ocean. One out of every four pelagic species makes its home there! But coral reefs are sensitive to water temperature. Global warming has heated the seawater. If it doesn't cool down, all coral reefs will die within 50 years.

Coral Reefs

A piece of coral may look like strange rocks, but it's actually a whole colony of animals. The hard, rocklike part is a protective shell. It grows around microscopic animals called polyps. It takes millions of polyps to make a coral reef. Coral needs its water to be just right. If the water heats up too much, the coral turns white and dies. This is called coral bleaching. The bleached part of a coral reef can never recover. The Great Barrier Reef of Australia is the largest reef in the world. It recently had its worst coral bleaching in 700 years.

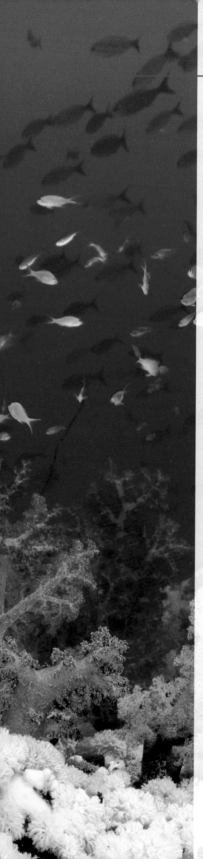

Turtle Tours!

There is a special beach near Tortuguero, Costa Rica. On this beach, sea turtles come out of the ocean to dig nests and lay their eggs. A few months later, baby turtles hatch and head back into the ocean. The people of Tortuguero used to feed their families by hunting the turtles and harvesting their eggs. The people were very good at this. In fact, they were too good. Every year, there were fewer turtles. They were in danger of becoming extinct.

The people of Tortuguero decided to do something different. They stopped hunting the turtles. They stopped harvesting their eggs. They gave turtle tours instead. People from all over the world go to Tortuguero to see the turtles. The people who live there run hotels, tours, and restaurants. Giving tours of fragile ecosystems instead of hunting and harvesting is called **ecotourism**.

The world is full of different ecosystems and biomes. Each one has a different mix of plants and animals. One animal shows up in almost all of them: humans. People like you are part of the natural world. And you are a part of the ecosystem you live in, too. You are a part of the delicate balance that keeps all the organisms in the ecosystem alive.

Ecosystems all over the world are in danger of falling apart. As a result, many plants and animals are **endangered**. This means that there are so few left that the species may become extinct. Both the great white shark and the panda bear are endangered.

If we aren't careful, we can harm ecosystems when we hunt, pollute, and expand cities. Our fate is linked to that of Earth's biomes. We must do all we can to preserve them. This means we need to conserve water and recycle plastic, tin, glass, and paper. We must find ways to reduce pollution and global warming.

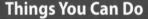

Things You Can Do

- **Reduce** the amount of trash you throw away.
- **Reuse** paper, jars, and boxes instead of throwing them away.
- **Recycle** plastic, aluminum, glass, and paper.
- **Clean Up** a local wetlands, park, or wilderness area.
- **Turn Off** lights that you aren't using.
- **Seal Up** drafty windows and doors at home.

Sea Mammals Drown

How do sea mammals sleep? For some seals, only half their brain sleeps. That way, half their brain is always awake to make them surface for air.

Dolphins often sleep while swimming. Adult dolphins sleep vertically, with their snout in the air. Or, they float at the top of the water. Baby dolphins must always swim or sink. A mother dolphin does not sleep deeply. She makes sure her babies surface for air.

Drowning poses a threat to the world's whales, dolphins, and porpoises. They get tangled in fishing nets. Since they breathe with lungs, they must surface for air. The latest study found that fishing nets kill about 300,000 sea mammals each year.

In this experiment, the jar is a freshwater body such as a pond or a lake. The fertilizer is the same as what runs off from treated lawns and farmer's fields when it rains. The sunlight is the same that would shine down on the body of freshwater in nature.

Materials

- freshwater from a pond or a lake (can use tap water, but it will slow down the experiment)
- two clean clear glass jars with a screw-type metal lid (16 oz. jar is ideal)
- liquid lawn or crop fertilizer
- floating water plants (tablespoon of algae from a pond works best)
- $\frac{1}{4}$ teaspoon measure
- masking tape
- pen

Procedure

1 Fill the two glass jars with pond or lake water.*

If you cannot obtain untreated freshwater, you can use tap water. However because tap water has been treated, it will slow down the experiment.

Bloom

2   Place a floating water plant or some algae in each jar.

3   Use the masking tape and pen to label one jar Pond Water and the other jar Fertilized Water.

4   Place ¼ teaspoon of liquid lawn fertilizer in the jar labeled Fertilized Water. Stir it thoroughly with the measuring spoon.

5   Place both the jars in sunlight.

6   Observe the jars daily, and record what you see in each.

7   After one week, place another ¼ teaspoon of liquid lawn fertilizer in the Fertilized Water jar.

8   Observe the jars and record your observations at the end of the second week.

Conclusion

You will see that the pond plants in the Pond Water jar are growing at a normal pace. The water beneath the plants is relatively clear. The pond plants in the Fertilized Water jar are growing rapidly and taking up all the space. The water below them is cloudy and murky. If there were fish in that jar, they would die due to the plant overgrowth.

Glossary

altitude—how far something is above sea level

apex predator—a predator at the top of its food chain, and is not preyed upon by others

biome—a large area that shares the same general climate of temperature and rainfall

canopy—uppermost layer in the rain forest, formed by the crown of the trees

climate—the usual weather conditions in a place

consumer—an animal that eats

deciduous—plants and trees that shed or lose their leaves

decomposer—an earthworm, bacterium, or fungus that breaks down dead plants and animals

desert—a dry, often sandy region with little rainfall, extreme temperatures, and sparse vegetation

ecosystem—the interaction between a community of plants and animals living in a natural environment

ecotourism—tourism to exotic or threatened ecosystems to observe wildlife or to help preserve nature

endangered—a plant or animal with such few numbers that it may become extinct

equator—an imaginary line that goes around the middle of Earth halfway between the North and South Poles

evergreen—a plant, tree, or bush that keeps its leaves throughout the year

extinct—a plant or animal that has completely died out; there will never be any more like it

fertilizer—any substance put on fields or lawns to make crops or grass grow better

global warming—the rising surface temperature of Earth caused by increasing amounts of carbon dioxide and other gases in the atmosphere

grassland—land where grass or grasslike vegetation grows; found in areas with hot, dry summers and mild, wet winters

latitude—the position of a place measured in degrees north or south of the equator

pelagic—relating to, living, or occurring in the waters of the ocean

permafrost—a soil layer below the ground that stays frozen for two or more years in an area where the average air temperature remains below 18°F

photosynthesis—a chemical process by which green plants make their own food

predator—an animal that hunts and eats other animals (for example, a toad is a bug's predator)

riparian—of, on, or relating to the banks of a natural course of water

taiga—pine forests that border the tundra; largest land biome on Earth

temperate forest—a forest that grows in regions with moderate temperatures

tropical rainforest—a forest with heavy annual rainfall

tundra—any of the very large, flat areas of northern Asia, North America, and Europe where, because it is cold, trees do not grow and the earth below the surface is permanently frozen

Index

algae blooms, 23, 28–29

altitude, 8

apex predator, 13

biome, 8–13, 18–26

black bear, 13

canopy, 17

caribou, 9–11

climate, 8, 13

consumer, 6–7

coral reefs, 24

deciduous, 14

decomposer, 7

desert, 4, 8, 20–21

Earth, 6, 8, 16, 18, 20–22, 24

ecosystem, 4–7, 15, 25–26

ecotourism, 25

endangered, 26

energy, 6–7, 13–14

equator, 8–9, 16

evergreen, 12, 18

extinct, 17, 25–26

fertilizer, 23, 28–29

gekko, 16

global warming, 10, 16, 24, 26

grassland, 18–19

hyacinth macaw, 17

Isle Royale, 5

latitude, 8

Meadow Argus butterfly, 18

meerkats, 21

Mojave Desert, 4, 21

pelagic, 24

peregrine falcon, 14

permafrost, 10–11

photosynthesis, 6, 9

predator, 4, 13, 18, 23

riparian, 22–23

recycle, 26

sea turtles, 25

taiga, 12–13

temperate forest, 14

tropical rainforest, 16–17

tundra, 9–12

wetlands, 22–23, 26

Sally Ride Science

Sally Ride Science™ is an innovative content company dedicated to fueling young people's interests in science. Our publications and programs provide opportunities for students and teachers to explore the captivating world of science—from astrobiology to zoology. We bring science to life and show young people that science is creative, collaborative, fascinating, and fun.